Carly Simon Complete

songs · pictures · words

Carly Simon Complete

Alfred A. Knopf, Inc.   Warner Bros. Publications Inc.
201 East 50th St.   75 Rockefeller Plaza
New York, N.Y. 10022   New York, N.Y. 10019

Photo Credits. All photographs except the following are by Peter Simon; p. 12, Tom Hanley; pp. 10, 11, 17A, 17B, 18, 19A, 19B, 20, 21, 22, 23, 24, 25, 26, 27, 28, 29, 30, 31, Richard L. Simon.

Library of Congress Catalog Card Number: 75-10582

ISBN 0-394-48753-2
       0-394-70625-0 (paperback)

Manufactured in the United States of America

First Edition

Design by Douglas J. Parker, Guilford, Vermont

Contents

Introduction

Long before Carly Simon became the "star" she is now, she had been photographed by her family, just for family album-type purposes. The photographs present a look at her life, devoid of the media hype that often characterizes the tonale of rock star photography. Here is a visual glance at Carly's life — little snaps from the past that, when pieced together, provide an interesting glimpse of the surroundings Carly grew up in and the changes she has gone through.

    The preadolescent photographs were taken by our father, Richard L. Simon, who besides being everything else, was also a brilliant photographer and who — much like any other proud father — loved photographing his family in the act of growing up. When Richard Simon died in 1960, I picked up where he left off, as it were, using the same equipment and darkroom, and continued the saga. My photographs of Carly reflect some of the love and intimacy I think we share, and the more recent photographs attempt to bring together the "star" image of my sister with the personal one.

    The photographs can therefore be appreciated on several different levels. At first glance you might see them as a study of one girl — Carly Simon — in the act of growing up; then you might see the collection as portraying more of an archetypical American girl, going through the process of acculturation, and view the physiological as well as the stylistic changes a human being undergoes through the evolution of time, regardless of who she eventually turns out to be. Thirdly, these pictures hopefully can be appreciated from a purely photographic point of view, going somewhat beyond the usual family album snapshots (and yet that's really what they are at the same time). Maybe a few of them can stand alone as works of art, using the phrase liberally. But above all else, you should be able to get to know Carly Simon as the person she is. Put these photographs together with her music and words, and you'll be closer to Carly Simon Complete.

Peter Simon

Carly
Interviewed by
Peter

The following interview was conducted over a period of several years, and choice parts are included here to make up a whole conversation. My sister and I have always been rather close, save for a few childhood years when sibling rivalry got the better of us, and a spell more recently when Carly has had less time to hang out. Hopefully, the quality of Carly's wit, the sparkle of her personality, and the love she has for her music, and the people she is closely associated with will come through this text as well as through the photographs that follow.

P: *Here we are on Midsummer Eve on Martha's Vineyard, and I'm about to do an interview with you for the long-awaited Carly Simon Complete book that we've been working on. How do you feel?*

C: *Medium to excellent.*

P: *It's weird to be relating to you, in a media-oriented way, rather than just shootin' the shit while driving down the highway.*

C: *All right, I'll close my eyes and try not to think that I'm anything but your sister, age four. You were just born; I hate you!*

P: *That's a pleasant start. When you look back on all the childhood photos which are being included in this book, what thoughts come to mind? Any particular memories?*

C: *Well, our father took all the photographs of me as a child. His technique as a photographer was very much like yours, in that he made you accept the fact that his camera was part of his attire. He rarely would ask anything of his subject, certainly nothing so commonplace as a mouth saying, "Cheese." We were all used to having our pictures taken. It was never a "dress-for-the-occasion" situation or something to make an issue of. And, therefore, what is telling is the expressions which were caught. No mirror faces. In the photographs of me, I see a lot of ingratiating going on. I think I felt uncomfortable around my father. I didn't feel positively accepted by him, and certainly I felt I was the least pretty girl in the house. When I learned to be seductive, I developed talents and interests I didn't know I had. Baseball was a strong one. It appealed to him because Joanna had music covered, Lucy had her dancing, and you were becoming interested in photography.*

P: *Yeah, I can remember you and Daddy constantly playing catch together on the lawn and going to Ebbet's Field all the time to see the Dodgers play. You were known around the block as quite the ballplayer.*

C: *The fact that I've never written a song about baseball disturbs me, lest you think I'm only kidding. Those were Dodger years for me and Dad, those years between 1955 and 1959 — those prepubescent years, when my interest in baseball contributed to my*

reputation as a "platonic" friend of the boys in the class. It never hurt to know Carl Furillo's batting average. Perhaps there is a song in all of this. But it sure didn't beat necking and other things, even though it was terribly important at the time as a mutual interest between Dad and me. I wanted so badly for him to be interested in me.

P: *How do you remember him now?*

C: *Well, he was incredibly compelling; six-foot-five, with sort of a poetic boy slouch, which made him seem more vulnerable. He was intense and delicate, totally charming with his wit, and occasionally tactless as a result of never having learned guile.*

P: *He was an astounding man. I keep hoping that some of his creative qualities and that commanding air have rubbed off on us, even though he died when we were both fairly young. Did Mother influence you a lot too?*

C: *I tried to write a song about her about a year ago which began, "Oh Lady, you were a mother to us all, you sheltered me from the cold, and if I accuse you of being wrong, then I was too young to know." It even got more sentimental after showing some sappy potential, so I rewrote it as "Grownup." She is and was the biggest influence in my life. I think the mother-daughter relationship is the heaviest. Boys continue to love their mothers but transfer their identification to their fathers. Girls have double-barrel mother: as love object and identification. Anyway, our mother — Andrea, as we call her sometimes — had all the accouterments of a lady who could have been mistress to glamorous men and of gracious plantations. She had the aura of being scented by gardenias. She was very petite but also wild-looking when she was young, and, as she has grown older, she has taken on an amazing resemblance to Katharine Hepburn. She is strong-willed and has the final say on most things; but she won't edit this, so "gardenias" it stays.*

P: *Did she encourage you to become a rock star?*

C: *She was very supportive of my musical interests; she always told me I had talent, and I guess I believed her. She also said that Lucy and Joey did too, which encouraged a healthy competition among us. I could have killed them both. But fortunately, through a simple twist of fate, Lucy had the really high voice, Joey was middle range, and I was low. You were always interested in parkways, the weather, and photography — and thus, no threat. I think we were all encouraged to develop our talents as well as we could, live up to our expectations. I'm not sure how much "fame" was involved; perhaps it was just respect.*

P: *I think fame was somewhat involved. I wish it hadn't been, actually. I seem to feel pressured into being recognized for accomplishing something, for contributing to society in some pleasant* way (as opposed to the mad bomber). But the motive for accomplishment is what confuses me. I'm not at one with this feeling of having to be well-known or successful. Sometimes I wish I could be happy to be anonymous. I think that fame is an ego trip that's not necessary (and usually distracting) to one's inner peace and light. Perhaps the fact that Dad was so famous in his day has affected me through osmosis. If I were a carpenter and you were a seamstress, would you rap to me anyway, and have it all appear in a book?

C: Only if you paid me.

P: Well, the actual singing and pickin' began in your junior year in high school. You just picked up the guitar and started strumming.

C: I was in love with Odetta. My good friend Steve Rosenheck took me to all her concerts in New York and got me into her recording sessions. I got a guitar. Lucy taught me some chords.

P: Were you shy about performing then?

C: Not that shy, really; I knew that anyone hearing me wasn't going to break or make my career. I sang for my friends, and that's really the way I looked at it. Later I began singing with my friends, and eventually with Lucy, which brought us much closer.

P: So how did the idea first emerge for you and Lucy to begin a career together as a sister singing duet?

C: It was after my freshman year at Sarah Lawrence. We wanted to have a summer vacation, and we wanted it to pay for itself, so we took a bus to Provincetown with our guitars and we walked the streets looking for a club to get a job in. There was this place way at the end of the road with dunes on either side; it was really a nice club. The man who had been the singer there had just been drafted, so we got the job — we were paid fifty dollars a week between the two of us, plus one meal a day on the house. It just about paid for our room and board, but we did get to go to the beach every day, and it was ideal for us. We enlarged our repertoire from one Peter, Paul and Mary song to five. We did a lot of Harry Belafonte calypso-type things, and then Lucy wrote "Winkin' Blinkin' and Nod." It was 1962 and the peak of the old folkie days; I couldn't stop hearing "Walk Right In" by the Rooftop Singers.

P: So then the Simon Sisters, as you were coined, got their act together and were finally encouraged to put out a record. How did that come about?

C: Well, when we came back to New York from Provincetown, we performed for Lucy's close friend Charlie Close. He was partners with Harold Leventhal, who remains a prominent manager (Alan Arkin and Arlo Guthrie). Anyway, they signed us;

we got a job singing at the Bitter End in New York, and that led to being on ABC's "Hootenanny," a big highlight. We were quite popular on "Hootenanny"; we were asked back, and finally "Winkin' Blinkin' and Nod" was released as a single and did well. I remember that being my first experience with "the charts." I was living with a boyfriend in the south of France and somebody sent me Cash Box or Billboard — I didn't know from either in those innocent days. "Winkin' Blinkin' and Nod" was number seventy-six.

P: Then, after two moderately successful albums with Lucy, you decided to venture out on your own. . . . How did that go down?

C: I met John Court and Albert Grossman (Dylan's old managers), who wanted to promote me as the new female Dylan. So I ended up making a record with them, produced by Bob Johnson, a song which Dylan rewrote for me with some new lyrics — "Baby Let Me Follow You Down." Robbie Robertson (of The Band) was the leader of that session. We got together and worked out the song; we recorded it a day later with what today amounts to an all-star cast: Robbie, Rick Danko, Mike Bloomfield, Al Kooper. I haven't heard it since that time, so I can't really comment on it now.

P: I remember that you recorded it around the same time as the Byrds revolutionized the folk-rock scene with "Mr. Tambourine Man," and your song had that same hard-edged twang to it. Why wasn't it ever released?

C: Well, Albert and John didn't follow it up. I guess they didn't think the record was very good, and they let me go; I got the "no-call" from them. I remember there were a lot of interpersonal hassles at the company, so I might have been a victim of that misunderstanding.

P: After that Columbia records gig fell through, did you give up and think you'd never make it again, or did you just sit tight and wait for the next go-round?

C: I thought I'd never make a record. I guess I never believed in myself very much, although inherently I must have had some sort of confidence. Otherwise I don't think I could have gone on. I did have a lot of support at the time from people like my family and some close friends. But I thought I never would amount to very much. I obtained a few typical New York City girlie jobs — secretary for a TV production company. And I tried to disguise the fact that I didn't know shorthand; thus I missed important parts of letters which I took hours to type out. The guy that hired me said quite readily that I was, in fact, the worst secretary he'd ever seen, or certainly ever hired; but instead of firing me, they promoted me to be assistant to the coordinator on the TV show they were producing called "From the Bitter End." I handled the talent.

P: Most artists have what is termed "The Big Break." How did that come about with you?

C: My friend Jacob Brackman, whom I had met a few years

previously while teaching guitar at a summer camp in the Berkshires, mentioned to me that there was going to be this dude coming to his house for a party who, he thought, was very influential, and he suggested that I just casually sing a few tunes on the sidelines and maybe he'd take notice. His name was Jerry Brandt, manager of the Voices of East Harlem and, sure enough, he got excited about me. Jerry has so much energy, and when he puts all this energy into one thing he becomes very vital; so he invited me to his house, he had me throw the I Ching and then translated the outcome — something about crossing high mountains and finally being happy in the plains. He convinced me he was the plains. He may have been. Anyway, he produced a demo which David Bromberg got together. Jerry took it to Elektra and Columbia. Clive Davis at Columbia passed on it, but Jack Holzman said okay and through Jerry Brandt arranged to have Eddy Kramer produce my first record, mainly because he had produced the Voices of East Harlem and Jerry was impressed with his work. The people at Elektra were very good to me; they were really behind my career at that time. Steve Harris and Jack Holzman in particular. Steve is the one who got me the gig at the Troubador, which helped a lot. I was quite heavily reviewed because I was the opener for Cat Stevens.

P: Carly, since this book contains most of your songwriting to date, I'd like to ask you some questions regarding your feelings about the songs you write, and especially the process involved in creating a melody and lyrics. For example, you seem to draw a lot of material from your childhood experiences. How come?

C: Many people ask me why I write so many songs about my childhood. In my seventh-grade English class, a certain rather imposing Mrs. Townsend said that when you write fiction write about what you know best. Draw from your own experience; there is enough of a world inside yourself. So I switched from writing stories about kangaroo children who were too large for their mothers' pouches (not realizing, of course, that was me) to more obviously autobiographical material, where only my name was changed — usually it was to Francine. I gave myself some artistic license: shapelier calves and fewer blemishes in general, but the family set-up was usually identical. I still tend to write about my most immediate relationships. Sometimes it's obvious, such as "Older Sister," and sometimes mysterious (at least to me), although we all know that the groom is the last to know — like "Embrace Me, You Child." That is a song which is apparently about my father, and the thing which is the clearest to me is how little I knew him and how clouded my vision is about our relationship. The most interesting thing about songwriting is the stuff you don't mean to write but which just slips out. It's a little reward of insight, like a particularly interesting fragment of a dream which you remember in the middle of the afternoon. I tend to write about things that are personal, and a lot of those things happen to be about the past. I think I probably dwell too much on the past. That's what "Anticipation" is all about, that annoying thing of always going to the former experience to see how you should suss the present situation out. The song is like a lecture to myself not to do that so much. But I still do have a tendency to go back for the answers.

P: So, do you write songs for yourself or for the public at large?

C: Well, the songs I wrote five or so years ago, I had no idea that they would eventually be recorded. So I was just kind of writing them just to write out things I wanted to say to myself, having no thoughts that anyone else might think of them. They were really just for me. Gertrude Stein told Picasso to paint for himself, and if the public likes it, fine; then you're a commercial commodity. If not, you're still being true to yourself, which is obviously the most important element. I've always liked old Gertie. But now I do consider my audience — probably too much. I'm more conscious of coming out with songs I think they might like to hear or could relate to. I want my songwriting to keep changing and moving into new turf with broader perspectives. Sometimes change is hard to integrate into creativity, though. You tend to rewrite your own songs. One of the things that anyone attempting to be an artist wants to do, or should do, is change seats, to get into a different space and write from a different point of view. I've always written personal songs, and that's okay, as long as my personal experience keeps changing so that I don't bore myself; it's important not to bore yourself.

P: The same is true with photography. I'll compose the same frame in my mind over and over — same lighting and composition, because I naturally tend to see the world in that perspective. Then I'll realize I've taken the shot before (with only subtle variations on the same theme) and won't snap the shutter this time. Then I'll feel frustrated or depressed because nothing new seems to be manifesting itself. Does that ever happen to you?

C: Sure. The thing I do is just wait, or do the dishes or play records until the inspiration hits or a "light bulb" of a new idea flashes in my mind. I like to write songs only when the urge to do so is irresistible.

P: Other than childhood, the major theme that runs through your lyrics is that of the male/female saga: the pain, the joy, the expectation or the fantasy of how it will be or could have been. Have relationships always fascinated you?

C: Definitely. You'll notice that most of my songs are about illusions in relationships: webs of half-spoken truths, things you can't say in time. The songs are an effort to figure it all out, or at least to free myself of the immediate dilemma.

P: "We Have No Secrets" seems a good example of that kind of song.

C: Yeah — the lady in question wants to know everything about her man, as long as it doesn't include anything she doesn't want to know. The idea of sharing every fantasy is becoming obsolete for me. The song made me realize in a concrete way how much I really would prefer to leave many things in James's mind.

P: *How is it to collaborate with Jake? How do you decide what to do?*

C: *Usually I have a melody and Jake takes a tape of it home, writes lyrics; we meet later—have tea, sometimes cookies, apple juice (Jake really likes apple juice). Then we watch TV and then Jake goes home.*

P: *That's great, Carl, but how about the melody?*

C: *Ah, well; you know.*

P: *Give me some more scenario.*

C: *After Jake goes home, he often reads—or so he says.*

P: *Interesting.*

C: *No, we sit down with Jake's lyrics, and he sings them to me over a tape of the melody; and I laugh because his voice is so original. And then I try to sing the lyrics, and if they work, it's a song. If it doesn't work, it's back to the drawing board, obviously. Sometimes the melody changes to fit the words or vice versa.*

P: *Let's talk about some of your songs, specifically. I suppose your most popular effort to date has been "You're So Vain". I know you've been asked this before, but I'll do it again for the record: who is that bit of bitterness directed toward?*

C: *I would say I had about three or four different people in mind when I wrote the song. . . .*

P: *Whose names will be changed to protect the guilty . . . ?*

C: *Yes, one is Melvin Hooshvitz and another is Bypress Fongton (that's the verse about Saratoga).*

P: *Who rented the Lear jet?*

C: *Henrietta. I actually did think specifically about a couple of people when I wrote it, but the examples of what they did was a fantasy trip.*

P: *Who thought of the bass line introduction, you know— blllooooop blllooooop. . . ?*

C: *That was the hand of Klaus Vorman, totally his idea. And a fine idea, if I may add.*

P: *Did you have ideas about the production before you went into the studio?*

C: *Right from the beginning, when I first played it for Richard Perry in L.A., we both could hear what kind of sound it might have. We sang it out together even before we went into the studio. Richard heard the mounting drums and had good ideas about the guitar, with Jimmy Ryan overdubbing it in a certain way. What Richard did was to sort of fine-tune it. The song needed that special tightness; it also needed a special drummer, Jim Gordon.*

Carly going over an arrangement for "Night Owl" with Richard Perry (at the piano) and background vocalists (left to right) Doris Troy, Paul and Linda McCartney, Jimmy Ryan (lead guitarist), and Bonnie Bramlet.

P: No Secrets was your first album with Richard, wasn't it?

C: Yes, and the most nerve-wracking—because I wasn't accustomed to his way of working.

P: What's that?

C: His concentration is bizarre. It's so different, but he doesn't miss a beat. He was often two hours late to a session. Made me furious. But he's so lovable you can't be angry.

P: And you got used to him?

C: Yes. By Playing Possum we were totally in tune with each other's habits. We have become such good friends from working so many hours together that we sit around, chew gum, and gossip when we should be mixing.

P: What did you gossip about?

C: Clothes, jewelry, people, chewing gum, erotic art, our sweethearts. A lot of advice has passed between us. Our vices have often been confided during vital drum overdubs. Also food. Rich and I are always thinking about the next meal. We make up imaginary take-out orders. He's smart, Richard. And one of the best producers ever, ever.

P: Speaking of Playing Possum, the album, how did the song of the same title come about?

C: Just wondering what all the folks I used to know who were into radical politics in the sixties were up to now. Ray Mungo in particular. I asked you once what Ray was up to, and the story line of the song follows a lot of what you told me. Wondering whether disillusionment had stopped him from pursuing his dreams, or whether there was something else churning around in his brain. Obviously, a lot was. His new book—"Return to Sender"—is fascinating.

P: How did Mick Jagger come into the act?

C: It was one of those things that just comes about sort of spontaneously. While we were doing the vocal on it, he just happened to call up the studio and ask if he could come down and visit. I said sure, and asked if he'd like to sing back-up, and he seemed enthused with the idea. He had a sort of twang in his voice, and I got into it. I slurred into it toward the end of the session. I started hearing myself saying "You're so vine," so on every successive verse I sang more "vine" than "vain." I had fun that night, I enjoyed myself.

P: Your first big song, "That's the Way I've Always Heard It Should Be," set you apart at the time from other women songwriters by adding a liberated consciousness to your work. How did people react to that one?

C: Oddly enough, some people thought it was a song about a girl who was so happy in her home life that leaving caused her such misery she would never be able to find an equally wonderful situation with her intended mate. Other people thought it was a perfect marriage anthem; and a number of people actually asked me to sing it at their wedding, because all they heard basically was the chorus, "We'll marry."

P: Did you feel at that point that you would never get married because it was a social bummer, and that you would inevitably get put on a shelf?

C: No, I didn't quite feel that way, although in my relationships with men, I've always felt that struggle. For example, "Slave" is timely in my life, because I do feel that way a lot: that I'm just another woman raised to be a slave; my conditioning is such that I am dependent upon another person, namely James. Yet I'm also quite aware of it, and aware of trying to change the pattern. That's the struggle of the modern woman who is trying to break those bonds, those strong promises that your mother and father give: "Well, you're going to grow up and find someone who will love you and take care of you forever and you will always be happy." It's the world glorification of the bride and bridegroom and all that society gives to married couples, which they take away from a single, unattached being.

P: Within the structure of the married couple, there can be equality and happiness, or there can be slavery. Do you think that woman as slave or each being a slave to the other is a built-in aspect of our human predicament?

C: Yes. But it applies to both sexes as well. I don't think "Slave" is a song that only a woman can sing. It's about people being bound to each other out of insecurity, with the feeling that they're not enough on their own, that they need someone else to complete them. . . . But there are two sides to the issue. A song like "Haven't Got Time for the Pain" represents the positive approach to relationships, where your partner helps you overcome those inadequacies. Both vantage points I feel are justifiable; it depends which side is more prominent at the time.

P: Speaking of relationships, how did you first meet James?

C: I had met him briefly in L.A. during one of my Troubador gigs, but around Thanksgiving time in 1971 James gave a concert in New York, and Nat Weiss, his manager and a mutual friend of ours, gave me a free ticket. I was hanging around backstage feeling a bit shy and uneasy, then Nat said, "Why don't you just go up to him and say hello? He'd probably love it." So I said to him, in sort of an innocently friendly way, "James, if you have any free time while you are in New York, why don't you ring me up and come over for some home-cooked food?" Then he astonished me by saying, "How about tonight?" I had made a date already, but I said yes to James anyway. I had had such a crush on him from loving his music, and I felt a little weird being with the man himself after knowing him from afar.

P: *The decision to get married, how did it evolve?*

C: *It happened about two days before we were married.*

P: *Could you tell me the details?*

C: *Well, I had just come back from L.A., really exhausted from recording* No Secrets, *and James had just finished his album* One-Man Dog. *We were back in New York together; there was nothing else to do. We had talked about it when James was in London and we both kind of wanted to. James had written me a letter in England saying that he had asked Mother for my hand. So we had our blood tests, and the results were immediate—since neither of us had the terrible Wassermann disease, we decided to get married. Then Nat Weiss sort of took over the preparations. He brought us in a limousine to City Hall, and some of the things that normally take eight days to come through Nat was able to just wave by in a day. So we signed the various forms and went ahead and did it in our apartment in New York with both our mothers—Jake Brackman was the best man—and Judge Ash. Actually, there was no best man, Jake was a good man.*

P: *When you married James, was it a really heavy commitment trip that you knew you were making for life, or was it just a spur-of-the-moment thing: ''Let's live for today,'' etc.*

C: *I felt very much in love with him. Neither of us knew (or know) what would happen; we just hoped it would all happen naturally. We wrote our own marriage contract, which included the possibility of us not being together, with stuff about what would happen to our money and offspring. I think we have a realistic impression of what marriage can be. Actually, marriage is a lot better than I thought it would be.*

P: *In other words, it's the way you always thought it wouldn't be.*

C: *It's so strange, but that song doesn't seem to apply to us so far. It's an example of how you can go from one space into another, and the things at one point in your life don't necessarily apply a few years later. And if you're sort of able to move freely, from one aspect of your life into the next, that's riding with the tide and going with the flow. I think that my marriage is the best thing that has ever happened to me. James is the finest man I know, and I don't feel trapped or like a caged bird. I don't think marriage is the answer for everyone, but it seems to suit us well. I think we both like the security of the other person's having made a commitment. I think only when you feel safe in love do you really relax.*

P: *Do you think the fact that you are both stars impedes your marriage, or that it actually brings you closer because it's such an amazing thing to share?*

C: *I think it brings us closer, because any conflicts there have been we've talked about and worked out, and gotten closer as a result. We also understand each other quite well; and whatever problems we have as a result of both being in show-biz and the spotlight, we share the humor about it and share the same perspective about it: mainly that it's not all that important.*

P: *Yes, but you must get caught up in the melodrama of the moment, though, such as getting upset because you don't feel free to do this and that career thing because James might get jealous. . . .*

C: *It happens sometimes, but especially now that we have a child, we realize the things in life that are important and those that are not; and stardom, as such, is really not such a high-level scene on the charts. It's a momentary gas and a flash in the pan for us both, for sure, but it's so much more basic in life's scheme to get along with people, be healthy, and know how to love and share all the corny things you've ever heard—right, Pete? It's true that in a situation where people are doing the same exact trip there is a lot of room for difficulty, a lot of sparks. There's naturally competition between two performers, and also between two married people; so we have a double competition thing going. We also could compete about height too, if we got bored with normal things to compete about. James is taller. But then again, I am the shorter of the two!*

P: *How do you think the production of Sarah has affected your career?*

C: *Well, I thought we should put a little more echo on her, but other than that, I don't think it will affect my career that much. Sarah is the most major creative event that's ever happened in my life; a lot of creativity went into her, and I have found it difficult to get back into writing songs at times. I think because my energy has been so devoted to her that I don't have that much surplus at the moment, which would normally be focused upon song-writing and performing. I'm hoping to get it back at some point. But when you have a baby, it's* SUCH A BIG THING, *you know, it's not like going to the supermarket and buying some food. Nine months of pregnancy is really a trip in itself. Labor is not funny, labor is quintessentially human pain, trucks rolling over your body. It's very heavy, and at the same time very high; it's really the highest I've ever been and, ironically, the most pain as well.*

P: *I already notice a similarity between you as a child and Sarah now, at age one and a half. I was often entertained by you as a youth when you made all those crazy faces, did cakewalks; I loved your animated personality, a thing you said was encouraged and rewarded often in your youth.*

C: *I can see that now in Sarah too. Like when she's cute or funny, I'll make such a fuss over her. I can see that maybe she thinks that's how to get her way, or that's how to win love, so she might try to develop that side of her personality. I should actually watch that I don't go overboard in that direction.*

P: *What happens if you're in your bedroom one night reading a magazine or two and Sarah goes by and watches you read and then goes into her own room?*

C: *I hope she gets a song out of it!*

P: *It does occur to me that performing was emphasized so much in you as a child — could that be a reason you are currently so afraid to perform in front of an audience?*

C: *Yeah, I think maybe because it was so important, the reactions that I got from my little performances. For some reason I felt I wasn't getting enough love from somewhere, and so I suppose maybe I did just that. It became crucial rather than just a little bit of fun and frolic. Whatever I did in the way of entertaining did become crucial, so maybe it stirs up that same thing in me now. I would love to be able to perform more often, and when I do it, I do get a real thrill. I like to perform to small groups, like ten or twelve people. I really think there is something unnatural about performing for a lot of people you don't know. A lot of performers I know do something to alter their consciousness before they go on stage. They either bring with them a glass of whiskey or get stoned beforehand. There's some kind of intoxication that precedes a performance which seems to help them through it. I wish something could work for me. I'm always aware of my body and how it's feeling. A lot of my mental energy goes into witnessing all of my body sensations, and because I can't figure out what they all are, my energy, when I'm anxious, goes wild.*

P: *I think many performers begin to lose the sense of doing the performance and, instead, are playing out a role that's actually being carried out from a higher realm; and they're just acting out the part, with little ego-identification. I think that concept can help.*

C: *I feel totally in-centered when I'm on stage; I feel dazed and confused. I wonder why I'm up there and what I'm doing and what's expected of me.*

P: *Well, personally, I don't think you should have to perform. I think the deaths of Janis Joplin, Jimi Hendrix, and other rock stars were linked to the pressures of the rock-and-roll business. They couldn't say no to corporations and escaped through drugs and, finally, death.*

C: *The relationship of drugs and rock-and-roll is interesting. I can totally sympathize with rock-and-rollers who use drugs, because there is this vast audience out there who is in love with you, and you can't figure it out — why it is so hyped. People relate to you as the media have pictured it, not to who you really are as a person. I mean, there are all these people who love you, it's just so unreal; and in order to get into that reality, you have to get out of reality by getting drunk or shooting up or something. Know what I mean?*

P: *It's true, but by choosing to be a rock star, you are really asking for it, in a way. . . .*

C: *Yeah, you are asking for it. There has never been an act in the history of man — except politician, maybe — that has attracted such large numbers of audiences. Concert halls are reasonably sized, maybe three thousand or so. But at rock concerts it can be as high as three hundred thousand. Now, that's a lot of attention to be focused upon a soul. I think it's a problem of energy. You're up on stage, and all this energy is being focused on you. And literally — just imagine all of it; even though you can't see it, it's still being directed at you, and it goes into all the pores of your body, into your eyes, through your ears, and, unless you can ground it, it acts like a bolt of lightning.*

P: *Certain artists find they can work with the energy. To me it seems that the rock-and-roll industry has created a need in its audiences now; so, in a way, they would adore anyone the media package properly. The illusion is that you're the one, whereas I think the energy is there anyway, and you might just be bringing it out in them.*

C: *That's so interesting, and it's probably right. For instance, I would be much less nervous about performing in a country where nobody knew me or could understand me, where I knew I wouldn't have to live up to anyone's expectations.*

P: *What does it feel like to hear your songs played on the radio? What goes through your system?*

C: *Well, it always feels intense. I can never take it lightly, it's always important to me; I want to stop whatever I'm doing, and there's like a momentary spasm of delight. I'm quite proud and a little bit humble. I am a real witness to myself whenever my songs are played on the radio. In fact, even though it's the same record that I've heard time after time, I somehow think that maybe something new will happen this time, like maybe I'll sing a certain phrase differently.*

P: *How do you feel about doing interviews? Is it a valuable forum through which the outsider can get a closer peek at who you really are?*

C: Well, I don't really like them too much, actually. My immediate answers are often flippant, contrived, half thought out. Rarely are they good enough for the questions asked. Reading them in print rarely gives the subtle inflections that give proper meaning. Also, something I say now and to you might not be true in a year; and yet, here it is in print forever. I am wedded to words for life.

P: I know that you've been unhappy in the past over certain interviews that have appeared here and there and felt you were quoted out of context, or whatever. Hopefully, that won't happen here.

C: I should hope not; after all, you are my brother. Recently, though, I did do an interview with Ben Fong-Torres for Rolling Stone. He was very responsible about getting things down accurately (which is the exception to the rule), but even then there were things which, taken out of context, appeared ludicrously beside the point. I said something like, "If I ever lose my sensuality, I'll become a cook or something." We had been talking about how I loved to cook, and I meant that if men no longer found me attractive, I could devote more time to cooking and getting fat. An example of an offhand, dumb remark growing increasingly fatuous and even reprehensible in the print version. I don't blame the angry women writing letters in with their reproaches. And if you feel life is too short to be wasted worrying about those women, tell me about it. I have never been able to decide whether to worry or not.

P: Do you feel a certain sense of responsibility toward your fans, or people who look up to you as a star or would like to lead a life like yours?

C: I feel an important responsibility toward those who consider me a star (as misguided as they might be)—people who might be nervous about meeting me or think my opinion on something is more valid because I am a singer or songwriter or appear on the cover of a magazine. I can remember back to when the situation was reversed in my life. On Thanksgiving in 1969, through some deviousness, I managed to be in the Stones' dressing room at Madison Square Garden. This was a year before I began recording my first album. Having an album out is what saves you from being an ordinary groupie. Most of us are basically groupies at heart, some of us are just more privileged than others. There's nothing wrong with it, but there I was, expecting the doorways to be too small to fit any of the Rolling Stones into their dressing room. When Mick Jagger walked through the door with extreme ease, he was like a diminutive version of a fantasy about him. Not that he is small, mind you; I think it's just something the media do with stars. I've got some interesting stuff in my journal about that night. Here goes:

I simply don't believe I'm sitting in the Stones' dressing room. Wasn't I prepared for this with Charles Addams, Oscar

Hammerstein, Irwin Shaw, and all the fabulous fauna of my youth? Mouth remains intact, but beyond the sound of silence. If I spoke, my I.Q. would descend further and further below sea level with every word. Danny (my connection to this event) remains cool, possibly moved, but discernibly collected. He is preparing his guitar for Keith Richard—seems to be going straight to work, is even jamming with the immortals. To do so is tantamount to seeing Abraham Lincoln in his underwear and remarking casually that his legs are hairier than you thought they were. Does it actually stem from self-esteem? Every time I accidentally glance (and it certainly has to be, as I am one of the genre that finds it necessary to be unfreaked when confronted by the upper strata), my eyes dart immediately elsewhere, usually to the cubes of muenster cheese pierced by feathered toothpicks. The self-consciousness I experience staring at the muenster cheese sets my eyes roving once again, this time to a magazine with a boring cover. If I'm caught there for over fifteen seconds, where in hell will I look next, back to the cheese?

P: So you must have some identification with the folks who just live to see you in person now, or flock around you after a show and want you to sign autographs. What a strange human phenomenon. What is it?

C: Well, the Stones are one thing, but people really do relate to their idols in a manner which they usually want to hit themselves for later. You become reduced to a chicken around a peacock. It's demeaning and humiliating, but somehow worth it all for the encounter itself and the anecdote which may later be told (and greatly enhanced in the telling). The prestige gained after the fact is as full of holes as sleeping with the football hero (if he's your type), missing the pleasure entirely and emerging smiling and full of how fantastic it all was. Soon, if you tell the story enough times, you begin to believe it yourself, which I guess is the idea. The script doesn't have to run like that, and I know I have made an initial "real" contact with people who previous to meeting I was in awe of and intimidated by. It's just interesting that I can't think of any of them offhand.

P: As a final question, would you say you have any major goal in life, as artist, human, mother, or wife?

C: Survival.

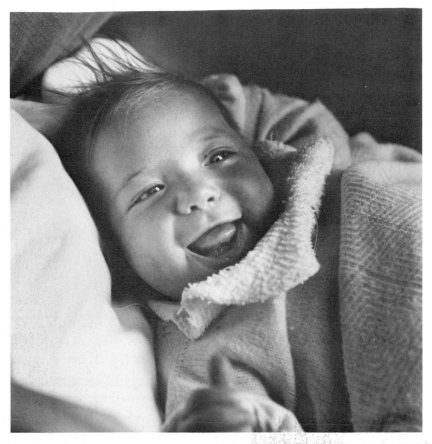

This is the earliest picture we have of Carly, looking not unlike other children of that age. She appears to be about one month old. **J.E.S.**

Cooling off on a hot summer's day in 1946 meant running under a garden hose and emerging victorious from the freezing spray. **P.S.**

Explanations
of Abbreviations:
C.S.T. — Carly Simon Taylor
P.S. — Peter Simon
J.E.S. — Joanna Simon
J.S. — Jeanie Seligman
(cousin)

Carly taking refuge with the comfort and love of her mother, Andrea. Gardenia it stays. **P.S.**

"How I adore Allie. She taught me all about Irishness and butterscotch pudding. I taught her how to be more tolerant of a cryer. She used to sleep with the chickens to avoid me." **C.S.T.**

At first, Carly wanted to be an artist, the singing came later. **P.S.**

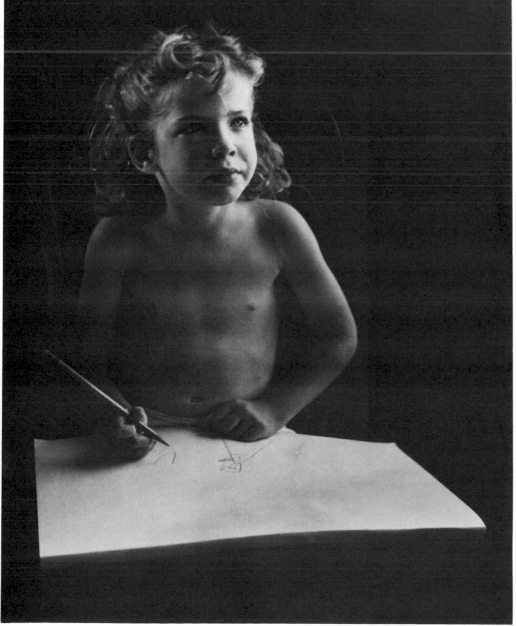

Carly wrote the song "The Best Thing," from her first album, after browsing through a bunch of photographs and finding this one. Here she seems to be turning six: "How was I to know, it was the best thing, to come along for a long time. . . ." **P.S.**

Carly's adoration for her uncle Peter kept her in stitches for most of her childhood, and her sense of humor and of the absurd was greatly aided by this companionship. Peter Dean now has two albums out of his own, with Carly singing back-up vocals on a few cuts. **P.S.**

The Brooklyn Dodgers were among Carly's first love affairs.
This photograph was taken in Stamford, Connecticut, where
the family had a summer home, often characterized by con-
tinuous baseball activity. **J.S.**

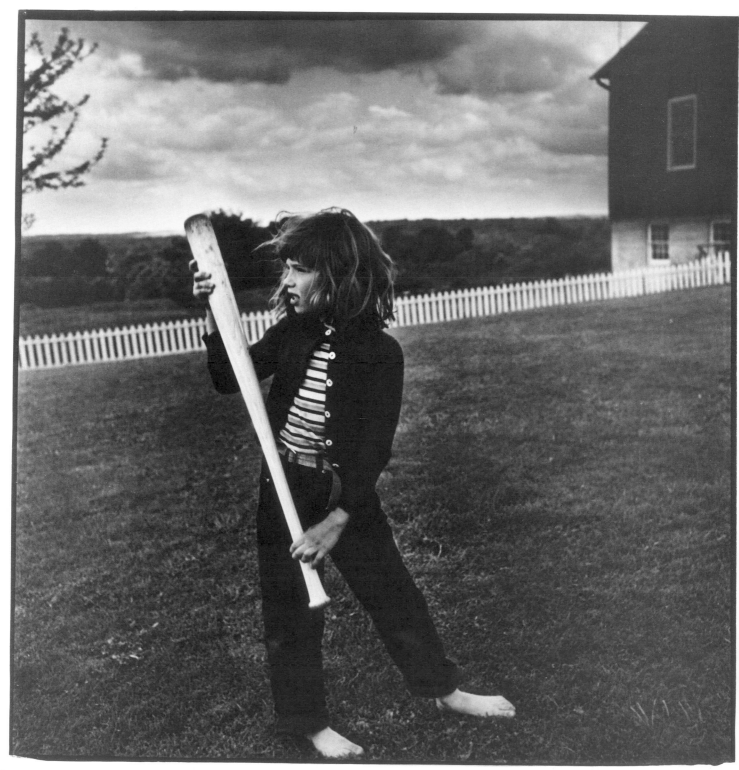

Carly with her older sister Lucy: "We were all into ballet, and even had little performances, which the grownups probably thought were adorable." **C.S.T.**

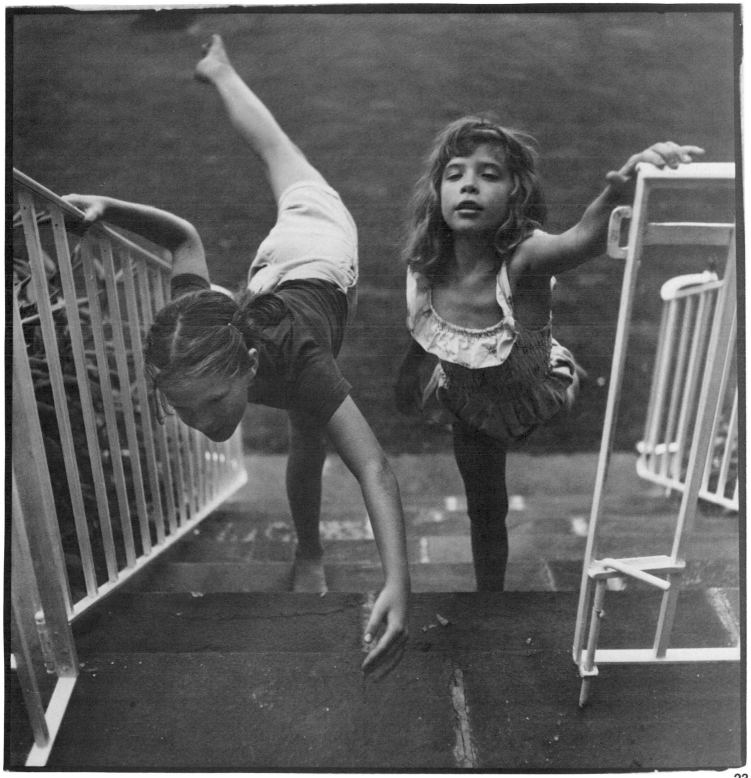

These are the three Simon sisters, two of whom refused to say "cheese" for their father, except for Carly, in the middle, too young to know any better. **J.E.S.**

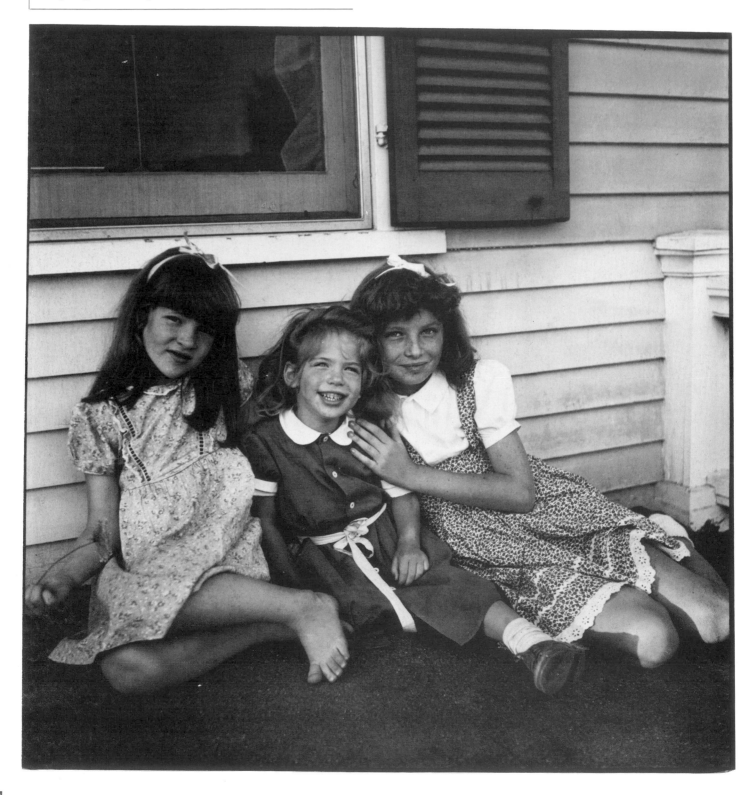

Carly, about age 8, with her younger brother, Peter, learning the basics of human relationships. **P.S.**

Carly during the missing-front-teeth stage. The worst thing about it was having to eat corn off the cob for an entire summer. **J.S.**

Catch it while we could—the Simon family, circa 1954.
Mother and Dad in the back; Lucy, Peter, Carly, and Joanna
in the front. Obviously no one's best phase. **P.S.**

"This may be my favorite picture of myself. I have a feeling if you watched me carefully for any period of twenty minutes, you could see me growing." **C.S.T.**

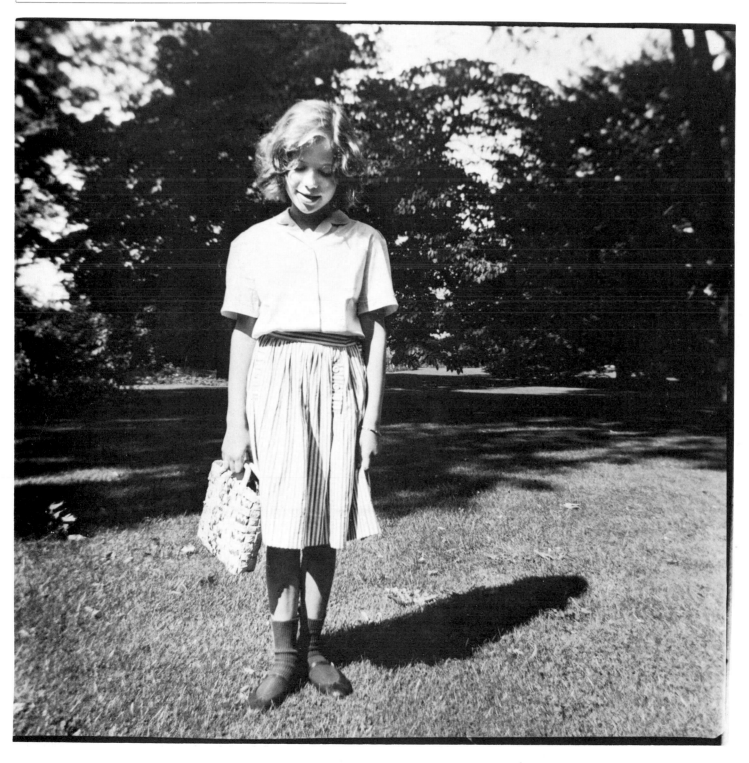

Sixth-grade graduation. Remember crinoline petticoats?
Whoever had the most was undisputed star. **J.S.**

This is the last photo in the book taken by Carly's father, and perhaps coincidentally the last shot of her looking innocent. **P.S.**

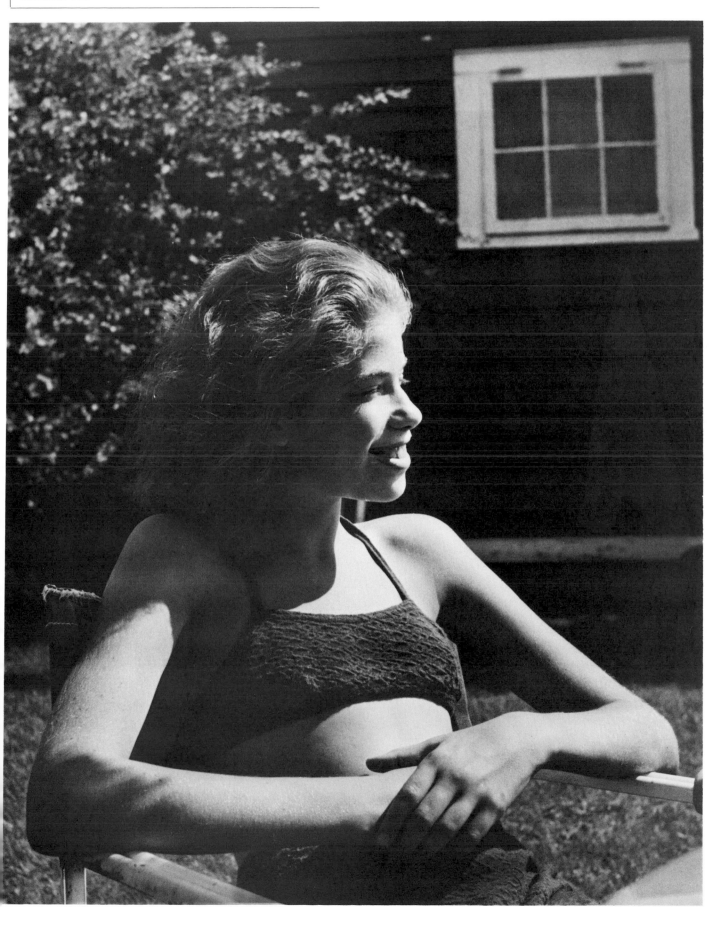

*The Simon Sisters: "Lucy and I sang together starting way
back when we first met. It was only later in life that we began
to do silly things like wear matching dresses. It looks from this
photo that we also wore matching thumb picks, and
knees."* **C.S.T.**

Carly's maternal grandmother was called Chib, but her other names included Elma Maria Chlotilda del Rio — and Carly has inherited most of them, as well as Chib's madness. Here she's about fifteen. **J.S.**

Carly has always been a great gesticulator, even when discussing matchbooks or pony rides. **P.S.**

A scene like this was quite typical during the early to mid 1960's, when Carly, Lucy, and Joanna would bask in the late afternoon soft-light, discussing crushes and grades, movie stars and Khrushchev. Bascomb and Laurie (dogs) would occasionally get involved as well. **P.S.**

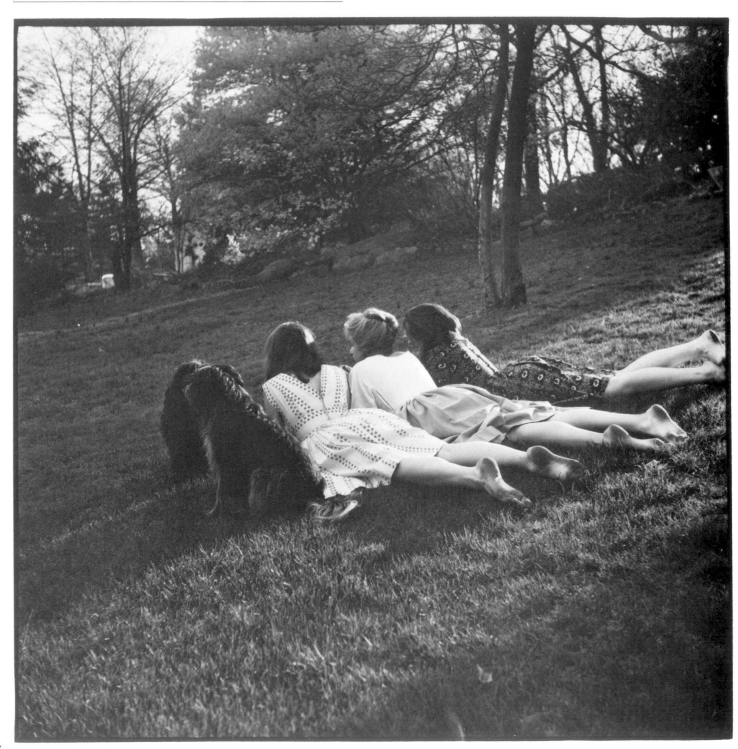

A cloudy day on the beach at Martha's Vineyard. **P.S.**

Backstairs in the house in Riverdale. I play the French movie actress who has just had a terrific row with her bacon and eggs. **C.S.T.**

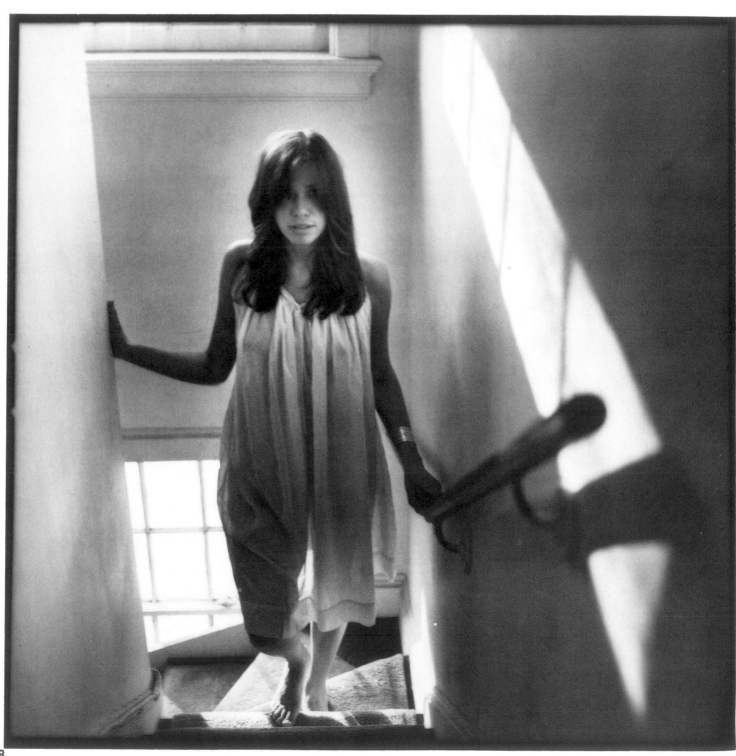

Here Carly is in the audience of a rock concert. "The obvious pleasure of the moment, magnified by the little tricks a good camera can do." **C.S.T.**

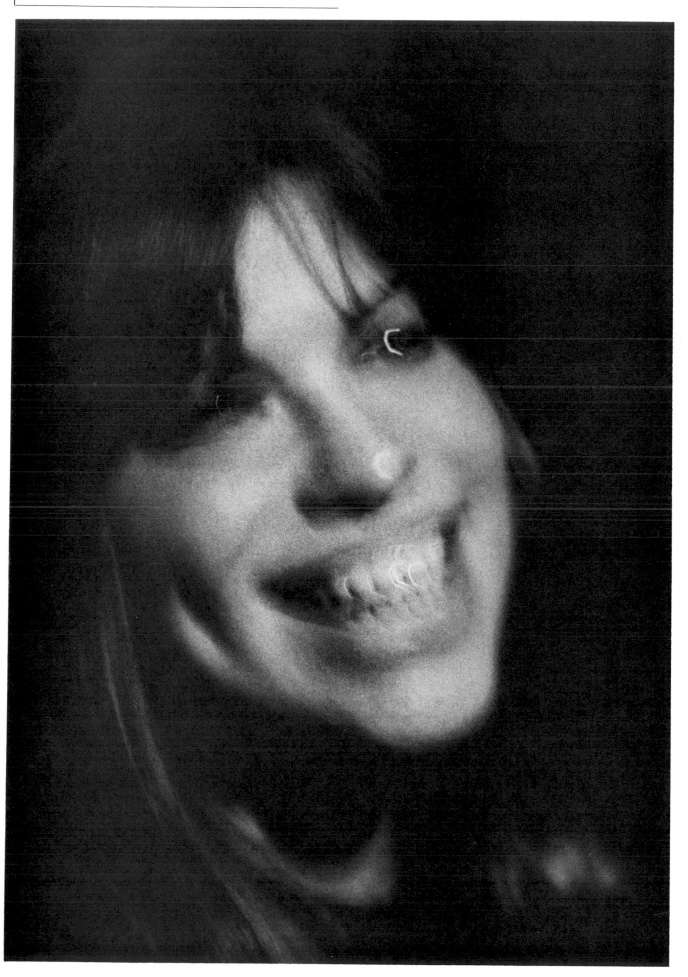

When Carly was in the process of recording her first Elektra album, she would commute from her apartment on the East Side of Manhattan to the Electric Lady studios in Greenwich Village. **P.S.**

When Carly was being photographed for the cover of her first album, a cat that she was holding (as a prop) scratched her breast badly. Here it is, doing it. **P.S.**

Carly with Kris Kristofferson, sharing a moment backstage during a concert they did together at the Bitter End in New York. **P.S.**

After the success of her first album, Carly went on tour with Cat Stevens. Here she's leaving the stage after a bow at Carnegie Hall, in 1971. **P.S.**

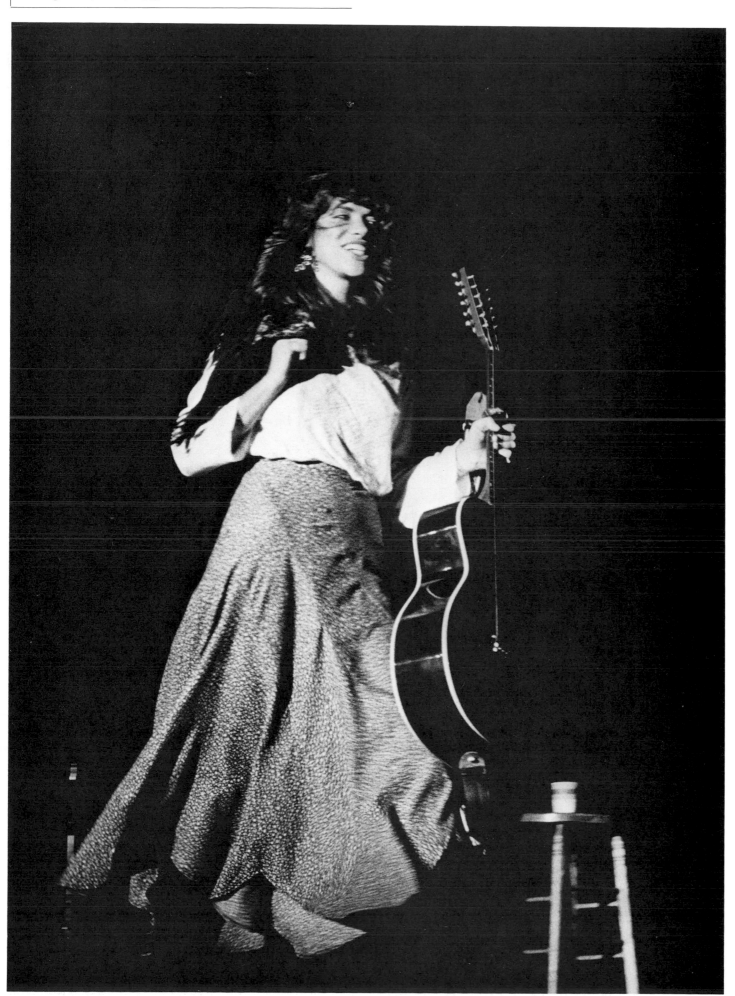

She did some concert dates with Livingston Taylor. This photo was taken in the dressing room (more like a men's locker room) backstage, exchanging some riffs before the concert. **P.S.**

The take (the following page is the outtake) for Carly's second album, Anticipation, *photographed at Regent's Park in London, which may explain the innocent pedestrian.* **P.S.**

With Cat Stevens in London during the recording of Anticipation. **P.S.**

Carly with the musicians she toured with, and who played on the Anticipation *album. They include Jimmy Ryan (upper right), Andy Newmark (lower left), and Paul Glantz.* **P.S.**

The honeymoon portrait, March 1972: "This day was exceptional in that it produced a number of pictures where leis were the only modesty I was allowed. It was in Hawaii, though, and late afternoon, and a post chi chi high involved my spirits so that quite the natural thing to do was to become bucolic. But I never thought it would make the cover of Rolling Stone." **C.S.T.**

This shot has long been termed "Carly and the Gardener."
Originally considered for use as her first album cover, it was
decided it wasn't quite the right image, but interesting enough
to include here. **P.S.**

Carly and James clowning around on their way out of The Hit Factory recording studio in New York, having just completed "Mockingbird." **P.S.**

One day Carly and I decided to take over the kitchen of a local hip restaurant. She's preparing a crabmeat salad for some unsuspecting customer. **P.S.**

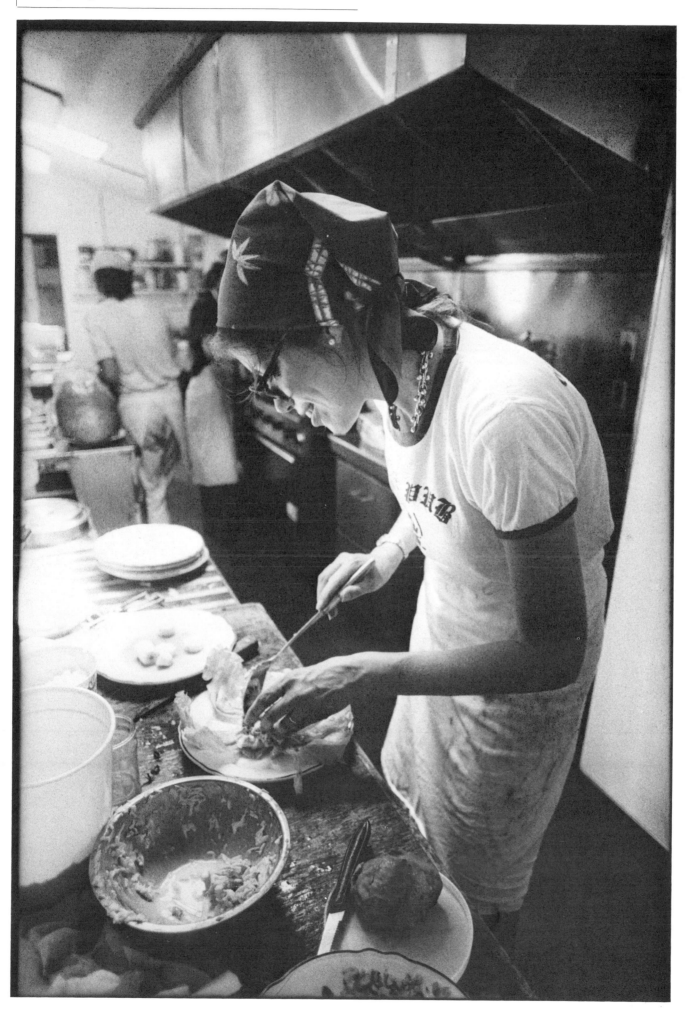

This photo looks like a still from a slice-of-life movie. It's a good-bye scene, with James about to drive off alone. **P.S.**

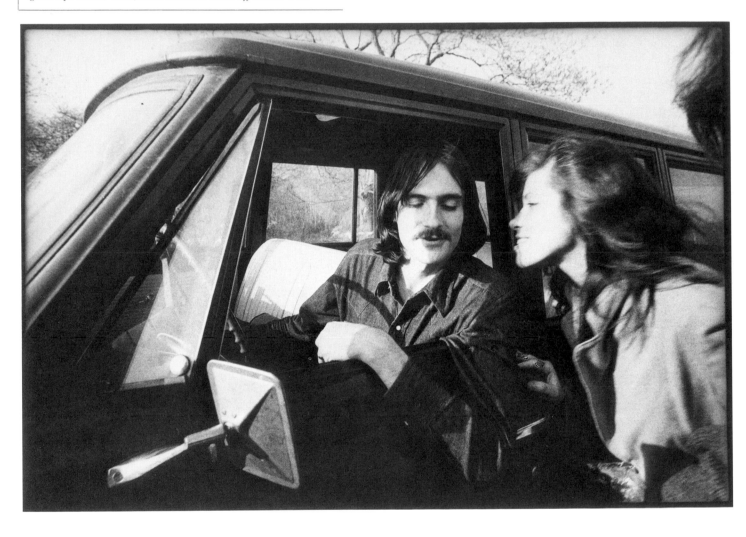

During construction of the Vineyard house. **P.S.**

During her pregnancy (which ended with the arrival of Sarah) she recorded Hotcakes. Or as she put it, "They're puttin' out too many phonograph records, I think I'm gonna have a baby." **P.S.**

Richard Perry (Carly's producer for the last three albums) looking over possible pictures to be included in this book. **P.S.**

Carly and James sharing the spotlight, on tour during the spring of 1974. **P.S.**

Involved in an eating scene, with a hazy coastal view as a backdrop. **P.S.**

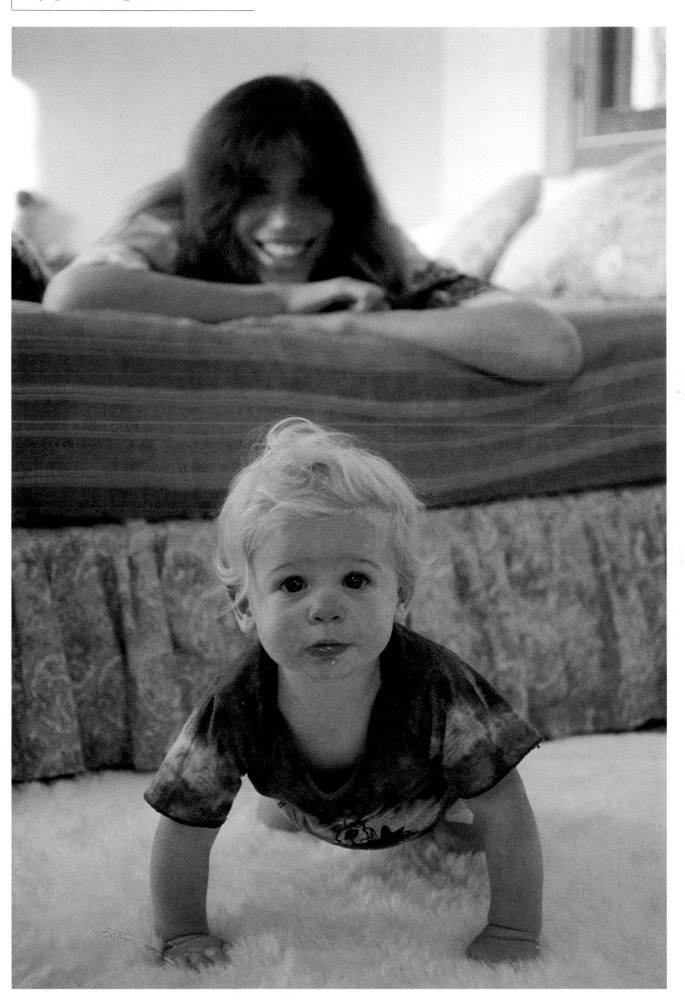

Playing with her daughter, Sarah. **P.S.**

Singing as duo at a Martha's Vineyard Benefit Concert in the fall of '74. **P.S.**

A recent study; she's looking out her kitchen window. **P.S.**

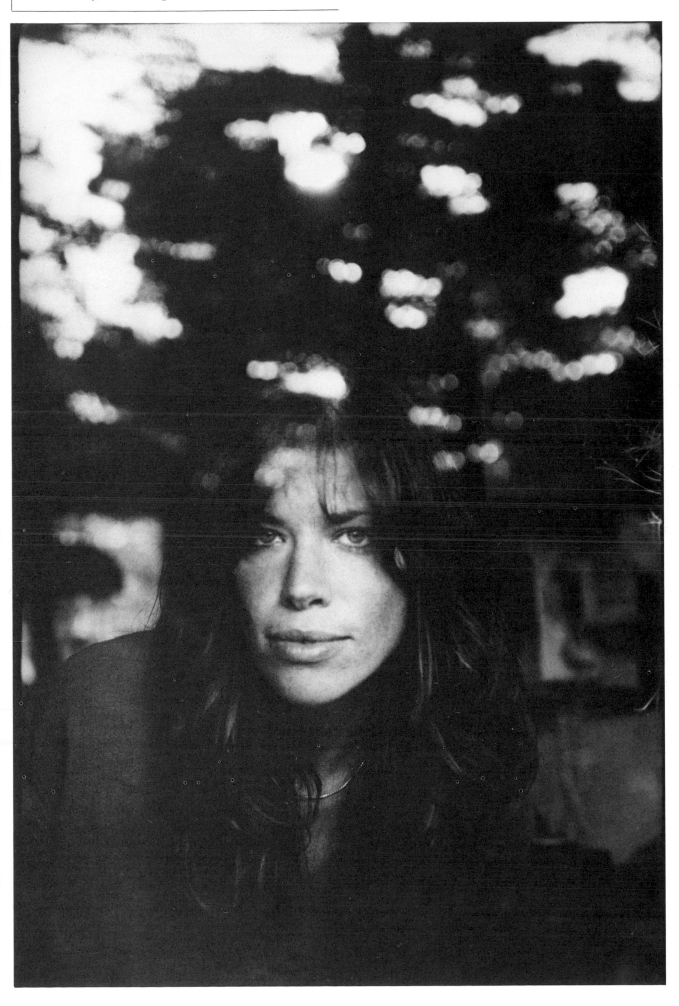

Relaxing on the couch, one of the few truly candid shots in this section. **P.S.**

Reunions

Words and Music by
CARLY SIMON
(Additional Music and Words by
BILL MERNIT and EDDIE KRAMER)

First one in the cit - y, wear - in' all those grass-stained
Next one at the old house, snow is on the
Last one by the high-way, wind blows through thin

jeans.
ground.
smiles.

Noth - ing is for - got - ten; ev - 'ry - one is pleased.
Pho - to - graphs and wine are passed a - round.
Some - one made a wrong turn, missed a joke by miles.

Some - one got his hair cut, the girls __ have lots to say. His
Some - one toasts an ab - sent friend, __ an - oth - er takes his seat. They
Some - one got her hair cut, a tear __ is in her eye. But

That's the Way I've Always Heard It Should Be

Words and Music by
CARLY SIMON and JACOB BRACKMAN

The Best Thing

Words and Music by
CARLY SIMON

it was the best thing ___ to come a - long ___ for a long
it was the best thing ___ to come a - long ___ for a long

time.

time.

What do the peo-ple at the end of the world ___ do ___ a-bout time? What a-bout

time? Oo, ___ oo, ___

oo, _____

oo, _____

ah.

What do the peo-ple at the end of the world _ do _____ a-bout

time?   What a-bout   time?   Their se-cret sleeps with   me. _____

rall.

a tempo

How was I ___ to know___ it was the best thing ___ to come a - long___ for a long time.

How was I,___ how was I to know it was the best thing_ to come a - long ___

Repeat and fade

for a long_ time.___

poco dim.

Repeat and fade

73

Alone

Words and Music by
CARLY SIMON

Another Door

Words and Music by
CARLY SIMON

that be - hind___ each new door is an - oth - er

1. door.___ **2.** door.___ An-oth-er door,___

an -oth-er door.___

Repeat and fade

Ah.___ Ah.___

Repeat and fade

One More Time

Words and Music by
CARLY SIMON

Rolling Down the Hills

Words and Music by
CARLY SIMON

Legend in Your Own Time

Words and Music by
CARLY SIMON

Moderately, with a strong beat

Well, I have known_ you since you were a small_ boy,

and your ma - ma used_ to say,_ "Well, my boy_ is gon-na grow up and be_

_ some kind of lead - er some_ day."_ Then you'd turn_ on _ the

turn _ on _ the

ra - di - o _ and sing with the sing-er in the band. _ Your ma-ma would say_

ra - di - o _ and sing with the sing-er in the band. _ You think kind of sad-ly to_ to you, ___ "This is-n't ex-act-ly what we had planned."

your-self, ___ "This is-n't ex-act-ly what you had planned. ___

But you're a leg-end in ___ your own ___ time, ___ a he-ro in ___ the foot-

lights ___ play-in' tunes ___ to fit ___ your rhyme. But a leg-end's on-ly a lone-

ly boy ___ when he ___ goes home ___ a-lone.

And though I ___

know you ___ still have the heart of that small ___ boy, well, you lend ___ it out far ___ too much, ___ and ___ no ___ one wom - an lov-ing you can ev-er feel that she's been real-ly touched. ___ Then you

Coda

Well, a leg - end's on - ly a lone - ly ___ boy _____ when he ___ goes home ___ a - lone. ___

Anticipation

Words and Music by
CARLY SIMON

with you; how right your arms__ feel__ a-round me.__

But__ I,_____ I re-hearsed__ those words__ just late__ last night

when I was think-ing a-bout__ how right__ to-night__ might be.__

An-tic-i-pa-tion,__ an-tic-i-pa-tion__ is

making me late,___ is keeping me wait - ing. And___

___ to-mor - row___ we might___ not be___ to-geth___ er,___

I'm no proph - et,___ and I don't___ know na-ture's ways.___

So I'll try_____ and see in - to___ your eyes___ right now,

The Girl You Think You See

Words and Music by
CARLY SIMON and JACOB BRACKMAN

names,   'cause I'm not nec-es-sar-i-ly   the girl you think you see.__ Who-

ev-er you want is ex-act-ly who__ I'm more__ than will-ing to be.   I'll__ be in-sane,__ a math-

'mat-i-cal brain,__ you Tar-zan, me Jane,__ to please_____ you,__   just to

please_you.__   I'm not nec-es-sar-i-ly__ the girl you think you see.__ Who-ev-er you want is ex-act-ly who_ I'm more than will-ing to be._ I'll _ be a queen, _ a

foul-mouthed ma - rine, _ your Mar - y Mag-da-lene, _ to please_ you._

I'll be a queen, _ a foul-mouthed ma - rine, _ your Mar - y Mag-da-lene, _ to

please_ you; just to please_ you; to please. _

rit.

Three Days

Words and Music by
CARLY SIMON

Lord, I feel lone - some, lone-some for the you I might, might have known. You'll be in L. A. in the morn - ing, and I'll be in Lon - don by sun-down. But when I sing, my song is filled with long - ing, and the

Share the End

Words and Music by
CARLY SIMON and JACOB BRACKMAN

hang on for u-ni-ver-sal dy - ing, please ig-nore__ the bay-ing__ of the hounds.

Save _____ me a place; ___ sur-round me with friend - ly fac - es. ___ All of us have

gath-ered here___ to share the end. ___ To watch__ the world__ go up in

(Group) Please, _____ Lord, we're not read-y; _____ give us some time _____ to work things
flames.

Our First Day Together

Words and Music by
CARLY SIMON

and all the plac-es___ in be - tween.___

Af-ter we'd spent nights to-geth-er,___ and breathed se-crets with-out words.

Af-ter we'd made prom-is-es___ that could _____ or might have

not been heard._____ Um,_____

Julie Through the Glass

Words and Music by
CARLY SIMON

just born a day a-go,___ and who knows___ where you've
been and where___ you're gon-na go.___ We
want you___ to love the world,___ to know it well,___
___ and play a part.___ And we'll

Summer's Coming Around Again

Words and Music by
CARLY SIMON,
JAMES RYAN and PAUL GLANZ

111

The Garden

Words and Music by
CARLY SIMON and JACOB BRACKMAN

You're So Vain

Words and Music by
CARLY SIMON

1. You walked in - to the par - ty like you were walk-ing on - to_____ a
   had me sev - er - al years_____ a - go,_____ when I was still quite_____ na -
   hear you went up to Sar - a - to - ga,_____ and your horse nat - 'ral - ly

yacht; your hat stra - te - gi - c'lly dipped be - low_____ one eye,_____ your
ive; well, you said that we make such a pret - ty pair,_____ and
won; then you flew your Lear jet up to No - va Sco - tia_____ to see the

scarf, it was ap - ri - cot.
that you would nev - er leave.
to - tal e - clipse___ of the sun.

You had one eye in the
But you gave a - way the
Well, you're where you should be

mir - ror as _____ you watched your - self___ ga -
things you loved___ and one of them ___ was ___
all the time___ and when you're not ___ you're ___

votte and _____ all the girls _____ dreamed that they'd ___
me, I _____ had some dreams, _____ they were the clouds ___
with some un - der - world spy _____ or the wife ___

be your part - ner, they'd ___ be your part - ner and
in my cof - fee, clouds ___ in my cof - fee and
of a close friend, wife _____ of a close ___ friend and

116

Embrace Me You Child

Words and Music by
CARLY SIMON

At night in bed I heard__ God__ whis-per lull-a-byes while Dad-dy next door whis-tled__ whis - key tunes. Some-times__ when I want - ed__ they would harmo - nize. _____ ___ There was noth - ing those ___ two ___ could -n't do. ___

___ Em - brace me you child, you're a child of mine. _____

___ And I'm leav - ing ev - 'ry - thing ___ I am ___ to you. ___

___ "Go chase the wild and night - time streets," sang

Dad - dy, _____ and God sang, "Pray _____ the dev - il does-n't get to

you." I thought to-geth-er they _____ must _____ sing the moon _____

_____ a-way. I thought that they must know each _____ oth - er

well for the mag - ic _____ that they made _____ when _____

they played _____ was-n't lost be-tween their heav - en __ and their hell. _

Em - brace me you child, you're a child of mine. _____

And I'm leav - ing ev - 'ry-thing __ I am __ to you. _

"Go chase the wild and night - time streets," sang

"Go chase the wild and night-time streets," sang Dad-dy,_____ and

God sang, "Pray_____ the dev-il does-n't get to you."

Ah_____ ah_____

_____ ah.

The Right Thing to Do

Words and Music by
CARLY SIMON

There's noth-in' you can do to turn____ me a-way,____ noth-in' an-y-one can say. You're with me now____ and as long as you stay,____ lov-in' you's the right thing to do;____

know you've had some bad luck with la-dies be-fore,____ they drove you or you drove them____ cra-zy. But more im-port-ant is I ____ know you're the one and I'm sure____ lov-in' you's the right thing to do;____

The Carter Family

Words and Music by
CARLY SIMON and JACOB BRACKMAN

His Friends Are More Than Fond of Robin

Words and Music by
CARLY SIMON

He's talked a-bout be-fore he gets there,_ though he can nev-er un-der-stand it.___ And I would like to be his a-lone, but I'm shy and can't de-mand it.___ But when Rob-in gives his

We Have No Secrets

Words and Music by
CARLY SIMON

The wa - ter was cold; __ the beach __ was emp - ty but __ for one. __

Now you were ly - ing in __ the sun, __ want-ing and need-

ing no one, __ then, __ some __ child __ came, __ you nev - er asked for her to come. __

She drank __ a pint of your __ rum, __ and la - ter when __ you told __ me, you

140

said she was— a bore, some - times— I wish, — oft times— I wish, — that I nev - er, nev - er knew — some of those se-crets of yours. In the name of hon -es - ty,— in the name of what is fair, — you al-ways an - swer my

It Was So Easy

Words and Music by
CARLY SIMON and JACOB BRACKMAN

When we felt hun-gry, we ____ would eat; when we felt
Now ev - 'ry ten - der fail - ure seems to o - ver -

glad, we'd ___ dance, ____ and when - ev - er we felt
throw old ___ dreams; ___ love can drive a nor - mal

drow - sy, we would doze. ___ It was so eas - y then, __
wom - an to ex - tremes. ___ It was so eas - y once, __

__ nev - er tak - in' an - y stands; __ it was __ so eas - y then, __
__ hold- in' hands with-out a plan; __ it was __ so eas - y once, __

else we'd be ab - duct - ed by the bears.___ It was so

eas - y then,___ nev - er mak - in' an - y plans;___ it was___ so

eas - y then,___ hold-ing hands. It was so And ___

Coda

___ Just hold - in'___ hands. ___

Waited So Long

Words and Music by
CARLY SIMON

Moderately, with a bold beat

Please _____ tell my sweet moth-er, _____

go on _____ now, tell Un-cle Paul. _____

Tell _____ all my girl-friends _____ not to wait _____ for me. _____

warm-est eyes — I'd ev-er seen.— He gave his lov-in' love— to me— the

way I've al-ways heard — it would — be. —

Dad-dy, _____ please for-

give me, _____ but I've al-read-y wait-ed so long. _____

So blow,_ blow,_ blow out_ the can - dles;_____ make my_ bed wide_ and long._ Tell all my girl - friends not to wait for me._____ Dad - dy,_

I'm no vir-gin._____ I said I've al-read-y wait-ed too

long._____ Dad-dy,_____

I'm sor-ry,_____ but I've al-read-y wait-ed so

long.

Repeat and fade

When You Close Your Eyes

Words and Music by
CARLY SIMON and BILLY MERNIT

close your eyes, __ do you see plac-es that you've nev-er seen, yet, you've been there? You've been walk-ing on the edg-es __ of a dream, and you're so__ __ much fun __ to be __ with. __ Big sur-prise! __ You've been in-formed __ you're not a-sleep.

Hard as you try, ___ you were nev - er real - ly meant to

weep. When you close your door ___ with a sign: "Do

not dis -turb," are you dis-turbed ___ to find that it's just as mag-ic as it

feels, and you're so ___ much fun ___ to be ___ with. ___

D.S. ☆ (instrumental) and fade

156

Think I'm Gonna Have a Baby

Words and Music by
CARLY SIMON

Moderately, with a strong beat

Plat-form shoes— on ta-ble tops, I think I'm gon-na be a— la-

would-n't be naugh-ty for the sake of naught ___ or be
pick me up ___ and you tune me up ___ and you

dif-f'rent just ___ to dif-fer, ___ I would-n't sell ___ my-self just ___
wind me up ___ and play ___ me, ___ you talk a-bout heart and ___ you say ___

___ to get bought or give just to de-liv-er. They're
___ you know soul and the way to treat ___ a la-dy. They're

put-tin' out too ___ man-y pho-no-graph ___ re-cords, I
put-tin' out too ___ man-y pho-no-graph ___ re-cords, I

Haven't Got Time for the Pain

Words and Music by
CARLY SIMON and
JACOB BRACKMAN

haven't got time for the pain, I haven't got room for the pain,

I haven't the need for the pain.

Suffering was the only thing made me feel I was alive,

thought that's just how much it cost to survive _____ in this world. _____ 'Til you _____ showed me

how, how to fill my heart with love, _____ how to

o - pen up — and drink — in all — that white — light pour-ing down —

— from the heav - en. I have - n't got time — for the pain, —

Just Not True

Words and Music by
CARLY SIMON

Moderately

You stick to me____ when I wish you gone,____
You're in my blood,__ a Ho - ly Ghost;__

you ham - mer on___ my thoughts through dreams.___ Your
I scream, but it's__ a hol - low plea.____ The

plot is thick____ with sau - cy____ schemes____ and
thoughts I swallow leave me____ thirst - y;

ways to reach my bal - co - nies._____ And I say I'm
you do a ver-y fine im-i-ta-tion____ of me._____ But I say I'm

not turned on ____ by the way____ you look,____ I'm
not turned on ____ by the way____ you laugh,____ I'm
not turned on ____ by the way____ you dance,____ I'm

not turned on ____ by the way____ you act,____ I'm
not turned on ____ by the way____ you smile,____ I'm
not turned on ____ by the way____ you laugh,____ I'm

not turned on _____ when you tell me that you need _____
not turned on _____ when you tell me that you love _____
not turned on _____ when you tell me that you need _____

____ me.___
____ me.___ But some-times,___ just some-times,
____ me.___

you can see the soft-ness in___ my eyes, and you

know_____ it's just not true._____

Grownup

Words and Music by
CARLY SIMON

Lyrics:

I stood in the door-way in my white night-gown; red ros-es on_ lin-en, I stood three feet from the ground. The grown-ups laughed_ inside, used words I did-n't know, but still I en-joyed the show.

They looked so love-ly, they looked so self-as-

sured, and I, just like them, would know it all when I ma-tured, and no

long - er be a - fraid of the dark-ness or the bears or the cracks in the

knees, feel - ing just as small__ as a this-tle in a breeze.__

But the child's i-mag-i - na-tion__ car - ried me__ a-

long and saw me through my song. See, I've

D.S. ⅍ al Coda ⊕

Coda

rit.

Forever My Love

Words and Music by
CARLY SIMON and
JAMES TAYLOR

Yes-ter-day's pro-jec - tion will nev-er real -ly know,___ but to - mor -

row's rec-ol - lec -tion will sure -ly show it was

so be -tween___ us. Ain't no oth -er way; time has

seen us___ day af -ter day. What shall___ I

Misfit

Words and Music by
CARLY SIMON

182

Come on home — with me, _____
Come on home — with me, _____

we'll turn on the T. ___ V.
we'll sit un-der a tree. ___

A-bout ten o'-clock ___ we'll turn off the light; ___
And if you get the itch ___ I'll sup-ply the scratch; _

___ not ev-'ry man — was born ___
___ not ev-'ry man — was born ___

Mind on My Man

Words and Music by
CARLY SIMON

Older Sister

Words and Music by
CARLY SIMON

Moderately

She rides in the front seat,
flies through the back door,
she's my older
she's my older

sis-ter;
sis-ter;

she knows her pow-
she throws French phras-

runs in-to some e-las-tic nights;_ so-phis-ti-cat-ed sis-ter sings for the soldiers of the soc-cer team, their sil-ver I. D.'s and so-ror-i-ties,_ they tin-ker with love in their Mo-del T's._ Oh,_ Lord, won't you let_ _ me be her for just _ one _ day? _____ She

Safe and Sound

Words and Music by
CARLY SIMON and
JACOB BRACKMAN

Strange times in Port - land, Maine,___ the
Flash from Mex - i - co:_____ the

lob - sters danc - ing on ___ the docks;___ Switz - er - land's___ been
tor - e - a - dors have all___ turned gay;___ Ro - man whores___ have

weird___ since___ they un - plugged the clocks.___
quit to seek___ a bet - ter way.___

Man and a wom-an in Brook-lyn Heights,___ each con-vinced___ the
Dope has un-der-mined the mo-rale of the Buck-ing-ham

oth-er's in the wrong, while last___ year the di-vorce___ rate tri-pled in___
Pal-ace guards,___ mo-tor-cy-cle gangs ride nak-ed down Hol-ly-wood Boul-

___ Hong Kong.___
e - vard.

If_____ through___ all___

___ the mad-ness we can___ stick_____ to-geth-er, we're

safe _____ and sound. _____ The

world's just__ in - side out and up-side down. _____

Ma - ha - raj__ wants you__ to lead a pil - grim-age

to Ti - bet;__ New York wom - en want me sound-ing off__ like a

Waterfall

Words and Music by
CARLY SIMON

Playing Possum

Words and Music by
CARLY SIMON

truth a - bout Un - cle Sam.___
hooked on a ho - ly man.___
live an eas - y life.___

We loved to be___ so rad -
But the wells,___ they do___
Well, are you fi - n'lly sat -

i - cal, but like a rag - ged love___ af - fair,___
run dry and the speech - es turn___ to words,___
is-fied, is it what you were look - ing for,___

and the
and the
or

some be - came dis - en - chant - ed, and some of us just got scared.___
woods are full of ti - gers, and free - dom's for the birds.___
does it sneak up on___ you that there might be some-thing more?___

Now are you play-ing__ pos-sum,__ keep-ing a low__ pro - file? Are you just play-ing pos-sum__ for a while?____ Are you just play-ing____ pos-sum__ for a while?_ Are you just play-

Repeat and fade

After the Storm

Words and Music by
CARLY SIMON

ex-pec - ta - tion of a calm af - ter ___ the storm. And your
set-tling like your weath-er-vane

bod - y feels so warm af - ter the storm. Ah. _____

Mm, _____ mm, _____

208

Love Out in the Street

Words and Music by
CARLY SIMON

throw out there.
call me Jez - e - bel.

All your ar - ti - facts___
'Cause I've come to know___ you
So let flow the hy - drants

in dis - re - pair___
I've come to know you so well___
and we'll dance in the spray,___

make up a pile___
from spy -
and we'll wash___

so high___ it could tie___ up traf - fic in the
ing on___ you from my bath - room win - dow in this
out all___ our dirt - y laun - dry in the

Are You Ticklish

Words and Music by
CARLY SIMON

Slave

Words and Music by
CARLY SIMON and JACOB BRACKMAN

Look Me in the Eyes

Words and Music by
CARLY SIMON

Won't you give ___ me that all your limes, ___
It's your ___ heat that makes me warm, ___

and I will give you a rea - son.
makes me climb on ___ you ___ like ___ a tree.

And I'll ___ rub them ___ on my ___ bod - y and
And I don't need no, ___ no fan-cy danc - ing

222

Attitude Dancing

Words and Music by
CARLY SIMON and JACOB BRACKMAN